2

er

TIME JUMP

BACK TO THE STONE AGE

Paul Shipton

Popcorn ELT Readers

Meet ... everyone from TIME JUMP

BACK TO THE STONE AGE

Emma lives many years from now.

Emma's **teacher** has got a time machine!

This is **Tim**. His friends from school want to learn about the Stone Age at the museum, but this isn't interesting to him.

The cave people

The cave people are from the Stone Age. They lived a long time ago.

This cave boy is one of the cave people. He does not understand things from other times.

Before you read …

What do you think? How are Tim, Emma and the cave boy going to meet?

New Words

What do these new words mean? Ask your teacher or use your dictionary.

flash

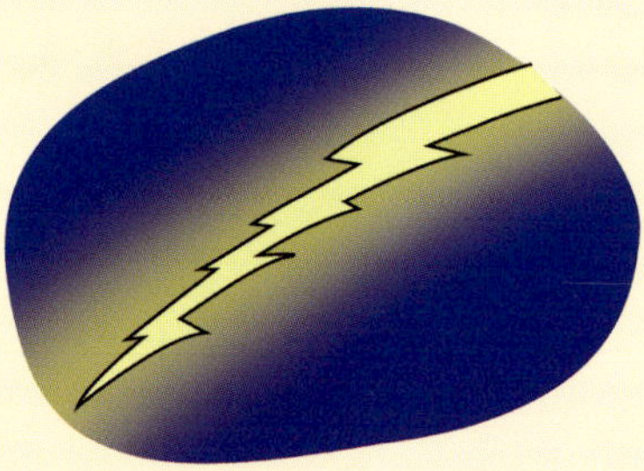

Suddenly there was a **flash** of light.

cave

It is dark in the **cave**.

glasses

Tim wears **glasses**.

fire

This is a **fire**.

grandfather

This boy is with his **grandfather**.

kick

She is **kicking** the ball.

museum

There are many interesting things in a **museum**.

picture

This is a **picture** of a man.

tree

This is a **tree**.

wood

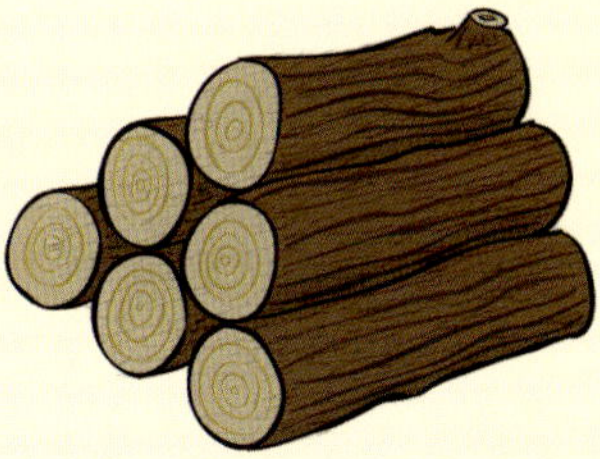

Wood is from trees.

'No way!'

Verbs

Present	Past
make	made
take	took
think	thought

TIME JUMP

BACK TO THE STONE AGE

CHAPTER ONE
Tim's First Jump

Tim was at the museum with his class. His friends liked it but Tim didn't.

Tim's friends wanted to look at the cave lion.

Tim wanted to play games on his phone.

Suddenly there was a flash of light.

Tim opened his eyes. He saw a *horrible* face in front of him.

'AAARRGHH!' he shouted.

'Why are you shouting at our teacher?' asked a girl. Her name was Emma.

Tim looked around. 'Where am I?' he asked.

'You're in our school,' said Emma. 'Today in class we're looking at old things.'

'Old things?' asked Tim.

'Yes - you!' shouted a boy.

'Why am I here?' asked Tim.

'You came in our time machine!' answered Emma.

Tim looked at the machine.

'Oh no!' shouted the teacher. 'There's a problem with it again!'

The teacher ran to the machine and started to kick it.

'Sometimes this helps!' she said.

Suddenly Tim saw a second flash of light.

There was a boy in the time machine!

CHAPTER TWO
The cave boy

The boy had long hair and no trousers. He was very frightened.

'Who's HE?' asked Emma.

'Is he from your time, Tim?' asked a boy.

'No!' said Tim. 'He's from the Stone Age. He's a cave boy!'

'Sorry, young man,' said the teacher. 'We can take you home now.'

The cave boy did not understand. Now, he was not frightened ... he was ANGRY!

He started to run and jump around.

The cave boy was quick. He was very strong too.

'Help!' shouted the children.

The teacher kicked the time machine again – a big kick this time – and …

'We are going to finish today's class now,' said the teacher quickly.

'Wait!' said Emma. 'I want to talk to Tim about something.'

But the teacher did not listen. She wanted Tim to go back to his time now. There was a flash of light from the time machine.

Tim opened his eyes but he did not see the museum. He saw trees.

'It's the time machine,' said someone next to him. 'There are always problems with it.'

It was Emma!

'I jumped into the light too,' she said.

'Why?' asked Tim. Emma did not answer.

'What's that behind us?' she said.

CHAPTER THREE
Back to the Stone Age

Slowly Tim and Emma looked around. There were cave people behind them!

'We're not back in your time,' said Emma. 'We're in the cave boy's time!'

She looked at the cave people. 'Are they frightened of us?'

'I'm frightened of THEM!' said Tim.

'Wait! They want to make a fire,' said Emma. Quickly she took Tim's glasses. 'Can I have these?'

She walked to the wood with the glasses. It was a hot, sunny day. Emma waited and waited.

'Yes! We've got a fire.' said Emma.

The cave people made dinner with the fire.

'They want to eat with us,' said Emma.

Tim looked at the dinner. 'No, thanks,' he said quickly.

After dinner the cave people started to sing … badly!

'I can play music on my phone,' Tim said. 'Listen.'

He had his phone in his hand.

The cave people were quiet.

'It's OK,' said Tim. 'Don't be frightened of a phone!'

But they weren't frightened of the phone ...

CHAPTER FOUR
The cave lion

The cave people were frightened of the animal in the trees.

It was a big, hungry cave lion!

Suddenly there was a flash of light next to Tim.

It was Emma's teacher, and the cave boy was with her!

Now the cave lion was angry. It opened its mouth and ran at the cave people.

Tim did not run. Quickly he played some music on the phone.

The cave lion was frightened. It ran away back to the trees.

The cave boy was happy. He took his new friends to his home in the cave and started to draw a picture.

'It's a picture of you, Tim!' said Emma.

Tim looked at Emma. 'What did you want to ask me in your class?'

'We wanted you – Tim Hopper – in our class,' said Emma, 'because you're my grandfather's grandfather!'

'Me? A grandfather's grandfather? No way!' said Tim.

He wanted to know more, but the teacher was at the cave.

'Time to go home!' she said.

Then the light was all around Tim …

He was back in the museum again!

Tim's friends ran to him. 'Did you see the cave boy?' they asked. 'He ran all around the museum. Then there was a flash of light!'

'That boy came here from the Stone Age in a time machine!' said Tim. 'And I went back to his time!'

Tim's friends laughed. 'Very funny,' they said. 'You were outside with your phone, Tim!'

Tim said nothing more about the time machine. 'I want to look around the museum now,' he said.

He stopped at the cave picture.

'What is that thing in his hand?' Tim's friend asked.

Tim looked at the picture and laughed. 'No way!' he thought. 'It's the cave boy's picture of ME with my phone!'

THE END

Real World

THE STONE AGE

The Stone Age started about 2,500,000 years ago. We use the name 'Stone Age' because people at that time made stone tools.

People in the Stone Age did not write anything, but sometimes they made pictures. We know about them because sometimes we find Stone Age things in the ground. You can see some of these things in museums.

Stone Age people cut food with this tool.

Where did people live?

Some Stone Age people lived in caves. Other people made homes with wood from trees. Sometimes they made homes with big animal bones. Often Stone Age people did not stay in one place.

These famous pictures are from a cave in the South of France. They are pictures of animals.

What did they eat?

They had food from trees. Also, some animals were food for Stone Age people. Stone Age people made fire and cooked some of their food.

How dangerous was the Stone Age?

Very! There were many big, dangerous animals at that time. Tim and Emma see a cave lion. Here are some other dangerous animals from the Stone Age!

cave lion

mammoth

woolly rhinoceros

smilodon

What do these words mean? Find out.

ground tool bone cook food

After you read

1 True (✓) or False (✗)? Write in the box.

a) Tim's friends don't like the museum. ☐

b) There is a time machine in Emma's school. ☐

c) The time machine takes Tim back to the cave boy's time. ☐

d) Emma goes back in time with Tim. ☐

e) The cave lion is frightened of Tim's phone. ☐

f) The cave boy is Tim's grandfather. ☐

2 Match the names with the sentences.

a) Emma	i) He is frightened and runs around the room.
b) Tim	ii) She makes a fire for the cave people.
c) the cave boy	iii) She kicks the time machine.
d) the teacher	iv) The cave picture in the museum is of him and his phone.

Where's the popcorn?

Look in your book.
Can you find it?

Puzzle time!

1 Look or read and write the words. Find the secret word.

1 

2 

3 This takes Tim to a new time.

4 

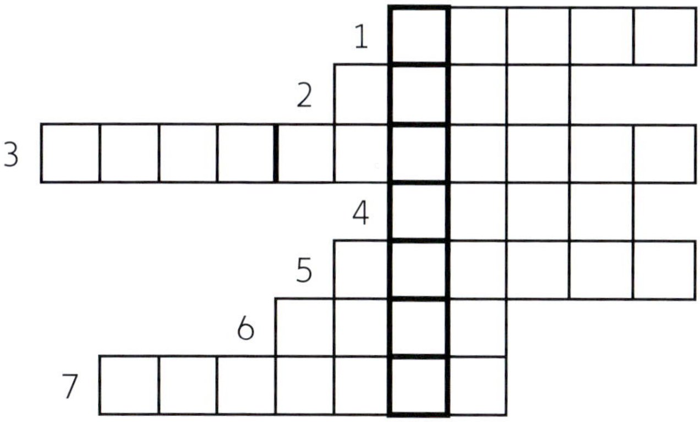

5 Tim and his school friends go here.

6 

7 

The secret word is ....

2 Work with a friend and answer the questions.

a) Who is your favourite person in the story? Why?

b) Who don't you like in the story? Why not?

3 Can you remember? Complete the speech bubbles. Now check your answers.

a

You came in our ....

b

There's .... with the time machine again!

c

It's OK. Don't be frightened of ....

d

Did you see ....?

4 Draw your favourite part of the story.

a) Who is in your picture?

....

b) What are they doing?

....

Imagine ...

Somebody comes from Emma's class to your class. Ask him or her questions.

Chant

1 Listen and read.

Into the time machine

Jump into the time machine.
Now where can we go?
Back into the Stone Age?
It's interesting, I know!

Not to the Stone Age!
I'm frightened to go there.
With big hungry animals
And cave boys everywhere!

2 Say the chant.